If I Lived In Spain . . .

To Jennifer, Dana, Lance and Derek,
adults all, but our children always.

Published by LONGSTREET PRESS, INC.,
a subsidiary of Cox Newspapers,
a division of Cox Enterprises, Inc.
2140 Newmarket Parkway
Suite 118
Marietta, Georgia 30067

Printed in the United States of America

1st printing, 1994

ISBN: 1-56352-168-7

This book was printed by Arcata Graphics, Kingsport, Tennessee

Film preparation and color separations by Holland Graphics, Inc., Mableton, Georgia

Jacket and book design by Jill Dible

If I Lived In Spain . . .

By Rosanne Knorr
Illustrated by John Knorr

LONGSTREET PRESS, INC.
Atlanta, Georgia

Spanish customs and words
Are quite easy, you'll see.
Just follow along
And pretend to be me!

If I lived in Spain
I'd have a new goal —
To speak perfect Spanish,
Called *el español*.

In the morning I wake.
"Buenos días," I say,
As I greet my *mamá*
And my father, *padre.*

BUENOS
DÍAS

Spanish word:	Sounds like . . .	And it means . . .
buenos días	bwAY-nohs DEE-ahs	good morning/hello
mamá	mah-MAH	mom
padre	PAH-dray	father

My breakfast is simple.
It's no trouble or fuss
To eat a roll or *el pan*
And fresh *naranjas*.

Spanish word:	**Sounds like . . .**	**And it means . . .**
el pan	el pahn	bread
naranjas	nah-RAHN-hahs	oranges
la leche	lah LEH-cheh	milk
jalea de fresa	hal-AY-ah dey FRAY-sah	strawberry jelly

Monday through Friday,
At my *escuela* in town,
All my questions have marks
That are turned upside down.

Spanish word:	Sounds like . . .	And it means . . .
escuela	ess-KWAY-lah	school
¿Cuánto es dos más cuatro?	KWAN-to es dohs mah-s KWAH-tro	How much is two plus four?
lunes	LOO-nehs	monday
martes	MAR-tays	tuesday
miércoles	myERH-kohl-ays	wednesday

"Who knows two plus four?"
Asks *el profesor*.
You can tell that I know
'Cause I raise *mi mano*.

Spanish word:	Sounds like . . .	And it means . . .
jueves	HWEB-ays	thursday
viernes	bee-EHR-nays	friday
sábado	SAH-bah-doh	saturday
domingo	doh-MEEN-go	sunday
el profesor	el pro-fess-OR	the teacher
mi mano	me MAHN-o	my hand

At lunchtime we take,
A very long break.
La comida's a big treat
Filled with good things to eat.

"Pongo la mesa."
I do what I'm able.
Mamá gives me the job
Of setting the table.

Spanish word:	**Sounds like . . .**	**And it means . . .**
Pongo la mesa	PONG-o lah MAY-sah	Set the table
Mamá	mah-MAH	mom

When I'm asked to help out,
To say I agree,
I nod up and down
With a great big *"sí, sí."*

(But if I'm angry or mad,
I say *"no"* with a pout.
The meaning's the same
As in English, no doubt.)

Spanish word:	Sounds like . . .	And it means . . .
sí	see	yes
no	no	no
la chica	lah CHEE-kah	the girl

In the kitchen, *cocina,*
I fix some food trays,
Cheese, olives, sardines,
And red *tomates.*

Spanish word:	Sounds like . . .	And it means . . .
cocina	co-THEE-nah	kitchen
tomates	toe-MAH-tays	tomatoes

I like *la paella*,
Chicken, seafood and rice.
And would I like more?
"Sí," I say, *"por favor."*

I play with my puppy.
He's small, *pequeño*.
When he chases his tail,
I just call him *loco*.

Spanish word:	Sounds like . . .	And it means . . .
pequeño	pay-KAYN-yoh	little
loco	LOH-coh	crazy

The library holds tales
Of Moors in their glory.
La Alhambra of old
Has mosaics and gold.

I read all the *historias*
From shelves left and right.
I learn of castles and kings
And a nearsighted knight.

Spanish word:	Sounds like . . .	And it means . . .
historias	ee-STORE-ee-ahs	stories
Don Quijote	dohn kee-HO-tay	Don Quixote

My friend tells a joke,
In a voice not so low.
The librarian looks stern,
"Shhhh. *¡Silencio!*"

Spanish word:	Sounds like . . .	And it means . . .
¡Silencio!	see-LEN-see-oh	Silence!
por favor	por fah-BOR	please

Ah, let's go, "*Vamos*,"
To *mis amigos* I say.
We'll save the library
For a rainier day.

I help shop for our meals.
I take time and go slow,
To choose the best foods
At the corner *mercado*.

Spanish word:	Sounds like . . .	And it means . . .
mercado	merr-CAH-doh	market
cero	SEHR-oh	zero
uno	OO-noh	one
dos	dohs	two
tres	trehs	three
cuatro	KWAH-tro	four
cinco	SEEN-koh	five

I count the fresh oranges,
One, two, three or more.
That's *uno*, *dos*, *tres*,
And *cuatro* makes four.

Spanish word:	Sounds like . . .	And it means . . .
seis	sayss	six
siete	syET-tey	seven
ocho	OH-choh	eight
nueve	NWEH-bay	nine
diez	dyESs	ten
frutas del país	FROO-tahs del pie-EES	local fruit
frutas de América	FROO-tahs dey Ah-MER-eeka	American fruit

"*¿Cuánto?*" I ask,
Then dig deep in my pocket.
To pay for tomatoes
I use Spanish *pesetas*.

Spanish word:	Sounds like . . .	And it means . . .
¿Cuánto?	KWAHN-toh	How much?
pesetas	peh-SAY-tahs	Spanish money
naranjas	nah-RAHN-hahs	oranges
la manzana	lah mahn-ZAH-nah	the apple

The clerk hands me my purchase.
I always say thanks.
It doesn't take much,
Just a big "¡*Gracias*!"

Spanish word:	Sounds like . . .	And it means . . .
¡Gracias!	GRAH-see-ahs	Thank you!
De nada	dey NAH-dah	You're welcome

Evenings at eight,
I dress in my best,
To make a fine show
As I stroll the *paseo*.

Spanish word:	Sounds like . . .	And it means . . .
paseo	pah-SAY-oh	a walk
pase	PAHS-eh	walk
¡Hola!	OH-lah	Hello!
¿Cómo está usted?	COH-mo es-TA oo-STED	How are you?
Muy bien	mwee bee-EHN	Very well

We greet our *amigos*
With a bright, cheerful smile.
"Buenas noches," "Good evening,
Can you talk for awhile?"

Spanish word:	Sounds like . . .	And it means . . .
amigos	ah-ME-goes	friends
Buenas noches	BWAY-nus NOH-chess	Good evening

My night meal is late.
La cena's at ten.
Except for a snack
I don't eat 'til then.

Spanish word:	Sounds like . . .	And it means . . .
la cena	lah THAY-nah	dinner
enero	en-EHR-o	january
febrero	feh-BRER-o	february
marzo	MAR-tho	march
abril	ah-BREEL	april
mayo	MAH-jo	may
junio	HOON-e-oh	june

June through August it's hot,
More often than not,
So after noon I just rest
And enjoy a *siesta*.

Spanish word:	Sounds like . . .	And it means . . .
siesta	see-ESS-tuh	nap
julio	HOOL-e-oh	july
agosto	ah-GOH-stoh	august
septiembre	sep-tee-EM-brey	september
octubre	oc-TOO-brey	october
noviembre	noh-be-EM-brey	november
diciembre	dee-see-EM-brey	december

With fast feet and knees
I kick *el fútbol*.
Each Sunday I play
In the nearby *parque*.

Spanish word:	Sounds like . . .	And it means . . .
el fútbol	el FOOT-bahl	soccer
parque	PAR-kay	park

Though I'm all tired out
From this running about,
I'm never too slow
To race for *helado*.

¡DATE PRISA!

HELADOS

Spanish word:	Sounds like . . .	And it means . . .
helado	eh-LAH-doh	ice cream
¡Date prisa!	DAH-tay PREE-sah	hurry up!

Many holidays, *fiestas*,
Give me time off from school.
I love costumes in colors,
Rosa, verde, azul.

Spanish word:	Sounds like . . .	And it means . . .
fiestas	fee-ES-tuhs	holidays
rosa	ROW-sah	rose/red
verde	BEHR-day	green
azul	ah-SOOL	blue

I dance the *flamenco*,
With wild, flying feet.
I click castanets
And stamp to the beat.

¡BUENA SUERTE!

From a balcony high,
I watch *el encierro*.
When they let the bulls go
Racers run *rápido*.

Spanish word:	Sounds like . . .	And it means . . .
el encierro	el en-THEE-ero	running with the bulls
rápido	RAH-pe-doh	fast
¡Buena suerte!	BWAY-nah SWAHR-teh	Good luck!

In the *Plaza de Toros*,
With his cape widely spread,
El matador knows the way
To make *el toro* see red.

Spanish word:	**Sounds like . . .**	**And it means . . .**
Plaza de Toros	PLAH-zah dey TOR-ohs	bullring
el matador	el mah-tah-DOR	bullfighter
el toro	el TOR-oh	the bull
¡Olé!	oh-LEH	Yea!

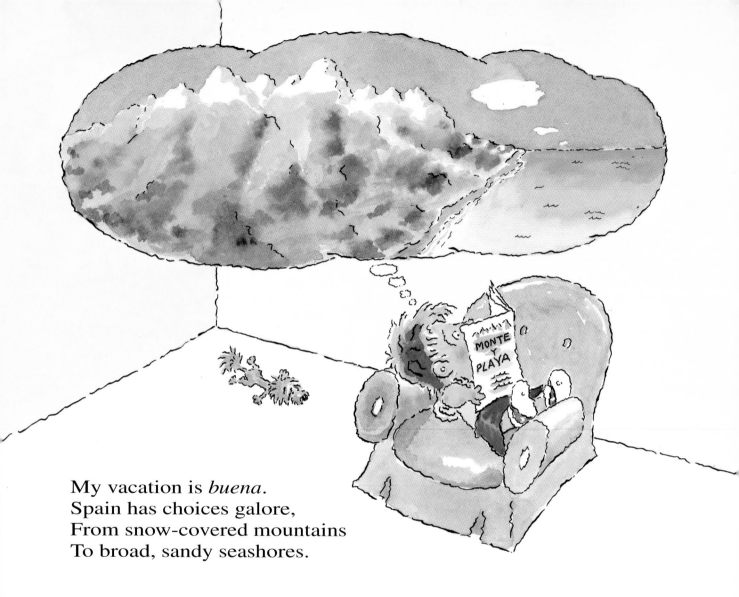

My vacation is *buena*.
Spain has choices galore,
From snow-covered mountains
To broad, sandy seashores.

Spanish word:	Sounds like . . .	And it means . . .
buena	BWAY-nah	good
monte y playa	MON-tay e PLY-ah	mountain and beach

To the north I can ski
In the great Pyrenees.
But I love the sea,
So it's *la playa* for me.

Spanish word:	Sounds like . . .	And it means . . .
la playa	lah PLY-yah	the beach
hotel	oh-TEL	hotel
restaurante	rehs-tow-RAHN-tay	restaurant

España, my country,
Is my special place,
With family and friends,
I say, "*¡Qué bien!*"

Spanish word:	Sounds like . . .	And it means . . .
España	es-PAHN-yuh	Spain
¡Qué bien!	kay BEE-en	How nice!

Spanish word:	Sounds like . . .	And it means . . .
adiós	ah-de-OHS	goodbye
amigos	ah-ME-goes	friends

Rosanne Knorr has won numerous creative awards and operates an advertising business in Atlanta, Georgia. **John Knorr** specializes in humorous illustration for advertising and editorial publications. Their previous book, *Atlanta: Welcome,* is captioned in five languages. *If I Lived In Spain . . .* is part of a series introducing children to the language and customs of other countries.